Retail Fashion Scenario and Strategy Planning

by

Charles Nesbitt

Copyright and ISBN page

Also by Charles Nesbitt

FUNDAMENTALS FOR SUCCESSFUL AND SUSTAINABLE FASHION BUYING AND MERCHANDISING

*

FUNDAMENTALS FOR FASHION RETAIL STRATEGY PLANNING AND IMPLEMENTATION

*

FUNDAMENTALS FOR FASHION RETAIL ARITHMETIC, ASSORTMENT PLANNING AND TRADING

*

FUNDAMENTALS OF FASHION RETAIL, TECHNOLOGY, MANUFACTURING AND SUPPLIER MANAGEMENT

*

THE COMPLETE JOURNAL OF FASHION RETAIL BUYING AND MERCHANDISING

*

RETAIL FASHION ARITHMETIC

*

RETAIL FASHION PROCUREMENT TEAM ROLES AND PROCESSES

*

RETAIL FASHION ASSORTMENT MERCHANDISE PLANNING AND TRADING

Table of Contents

PREFACE

The process of buying and selling in some form or other of goods has been with us since time immemorial. Often when one stands in bewilderment in an elegant shopping mall and wonder how all the stores are able to effectively seduce the many shoppers trawling the wide corridors to readily part with their well-earned money while at the same time enabling them to possibly enjoy a wonderful social experience.

The plan of offering goods to the potential customer is a complicated one and is a science that involves many players whose individual contributions slot seamlessly together and are so perfectly co-ordinated that it provides the perception that it is the result of one individual concerted effort.

In order that this is most effectively done requires careful planning and formulation of a chain of events that are designed to deliver the envisioned objectives that will guarantee the development of a successful and sustainable business. An ideal saying is "if you do not know where you are going you may well end up somewhere else".

The reality is that we exist in a time that is complex, risky while also opportunistic but with more hostile competitors change happens more frequently with the result that it is becoming harder to manage businesses with increased workloads and challenges making it important to take quicker decisions.

It is therefore imperative that having a concise strategy in place helps to focus on the right customers and to link the philosophies and values to the customers and stakeholders in such a way that it is sustainable over the longer term. The strategy informs, focuses attention and inspires performance. It should be simple, clear and compelling while still being multifaceted and challenging. Consistency is absolutely vital to provide the road map to be followed by the operational and tactical planned activities. If these principles are not strictly adhered to in all likelihood the unsuccessful execution of the strategy can be the unpleasant consequence.

In order to avoid this happening there needs to be a pre-planned setting of goals that are realistic, specific and quantifiable that are achieved via a set design of tactical operational actions. Strategy can be described as a basic process that leads change in the business. To do this a view of the future is required in order to know what needs to be done to operate in the new world. The end result should be the addition of sustainable value to the customer which will ensure the survival and future success of the organisation.

Leading companies are well aware that to maintain the competitive edge and achieve success they need to have an effective strategic plan in place.

This book endeavours to try and outline the rudimentary key principles and mechanisms by which this happens and should be helpful to students, people in retailing and those who are maybe considering a career in the industry. For those who already are part of the fashion buying and merchandising community this book will be beneficial in that it provides a complete simplified overview of all the integral activities and roles that go to make up the topic and thereby will provide a broader insight into their own career.

The material of the book, other than that specifically referenced is the result of the author's own exposure to the subject during a career spanning thirty five years at a major retail organisation in Southern Africa, the support from colleagues, mentors, interaction with suppliers and own research. There has been some cross referencing to other books or technical material but the book focuses largely at a higher level on the key principles, concepts and theories and hence there is none or very little mention of retailers by name or technological packages for some key activities such as planning, allocating, critical path management, logistics and the like.

INTRODUCTION

It is always difficult to accomplish anything without a plan. Whether it is a sporting event, a dinner, preparing a lecture or managing a business, a strategic plan is required. The strategic plan enables business leaders to prioritise where to spend time, human resources and financial capital in order to deliver the best outcomes.

The action is implemented through the use of specific and measurable objectives together with tactics to ensure that the clearly stated mission as to why the company exists is achieved. A point to note is that the more adventurous the strategy, the higher is the risk involved but may still reap more reward. It is important therefore to reiterate that the mission must be realistic and adaptable.

While it is acknowledged the strategic plans are required to be flexible in order to maintain the best possible competitive advantage and adapt to achieve their set down objectives there are unchanging values of the company that exist to serve as a point of reference to provide guidance in the process of strategic decision making. These primary ideals form the vision of the company and are expressed in the mission statement which communicates the ideology of the company remaining relatively constant. In short it is the reason for the existence of the firm and outlines the visionary goals which will be pursued in order that the mission will be achieved. The strategic plan answers the question as to why which differs from the business or operational plan which answers the question how. The objectives and tactics required in order to achieve the strategic plan will be reflected in an operational plan. It must be noted that even if the core business activities change completely, the ideologies of the company will remain unchanged. Examples of core values are integrity, innovation, good customer service and social responsibility.

The purpose or reason for the existence of the company is also likely to remain unchanged, for example, a main reason for existence of a company is most likely to make a profit but what is important is the definition of how the profit will be generated and should portray the firm as it really is.

The visionary goals of the company which are selected by management are normally at a relatively high level and are probably in the long term that the company will continually strive for. Such goals can be quantitative but may also be more general. Such as an example could be to strive to be seen as the foremost leader in its field.

A standstill assessment of the current status will identify what needs to change and that which is not performing. The purpose will be to establish where the focus should be applied and question if the current incumbents being held responsible are the most suitable and whether or not additional resources are required.

A strategic plan is required to cater for the consistently changing and more complex environments which need to be identified through detailed strengths, weaknesses, opportunities and threats analysis of both internal and external factors. Examples of these may be a stable internal infrastructure, exchange rate fluctuations, and new competitor activity, potential new markets and the like. The plan should provide a view of the future so it is clear as to what the business is required to do in order to survive in the new world and best serve the customer in a consistent manner.

While it is great to have a strategic plan, it is equally important that the plan is regularly reviewed and updated and is followed relentlessly. For this to happen effectively the format has to be efficient, flexible and interactive. As planning is an ongoing process, so the setup must allow for information to be captured, shared and updated in real time which will alert the retailer to the warning signs as to what could happen in particular situations and have alternative ideas readily in place that can be easily and quickly implemented.

SCENARIO PLANNING

From a broader perspective it is wise to evaluate the forecasts of your own and respected scenario planners to attempt to understand any possible impacts on the business and trading environment that may or may not evolve in the future. Scenario analysis is used to formulate a picture of the potential trading landscape in the longer term. Previously strategic planning was almost simply the financial extrapolation of past history going forward with hardly any qualitative discussion about the social conditions where the combined effect of various factors can have a significant impact. Some of these that we think we know about are forward trends, demographic shifts and the impact of new technologies. Those which we have no knowledge of are the uncertainties which are almost unpredictable such as currency rates, interest rates, outcomes of elections, impact of dominant political leaders, effect of political sanctions and the road ahead in terms of high risk hotspots such as the circumstances currently being experienced in the middle east, the consequence of an overwhelming influx of refugees into various countries, fads and fashions and technological innovations.

The changing of the way we work

There is a well-worn saying about change and that is certain is that there will be change. In talking about change it is unusual to understand what is unlikely to change and there are elements that will not change in the near future.

Included in these elements are items such as certainty where we know we need assurance that it is possible to avoid pain and gain pleasure. A basic need is also that we need variety to keep up the levels of stimulation through continuous change as well the desire to feel significant through recognition and develop a feeling of belonging or being loved and respected. The need to continually wishing to grow and expand our capacities and capabilities will never change and the contribution that we make will satisfy the sense of delivering to the best of our ability. Building a feeling of trust amongst all those with whom we interact is a major factor. All these elements will remain static while the environment wherein we operate will without doubt keep on changing on a continuous basis.

The way we work in the longer term is highly likely to dramatically change. There is no dispute that the manner in which tasks are completed is rapidly adapting to suit a totally new environment. The advancement of technology, connectivity and the expectations of both employers and employees are demanding that the economic activities be radically reviewed.

There is an ever increasing trend to relocate resources from the traditional high density centres such as Hong Kong, Tokyo, London, Paris and the like because of high living costs, fast increasing rentals, and salaries which are being outpaced by costs. As a result the purchasing power of residents is being severely diminished and therefore this tendency is forcing organisations to relocate to areas where it is cheaper to live and conduct business. Technology has aided this process as it is easier to operate from remoter areas and still have access through tools such as Google, Dropbox, Skype and the like which makes it just as easy to service customers as effectively no matter where the base location is. The base link ups could also be temporary in that desks could be rented with all the required technological facilities, boardroom or conference facilities supported by the appropriate equipment and catering requirements thus saving investment in permanent structures.

Apart from being able to conveniently work from different sites the necessity for a substantial portion of the workforce no longer have to negotiate the traffic or use public transport daily and therefore the surplus time saving can be productively utilised. There are instances that those firms who find it difficult to adapt to this newer culture and stubbornly maintain a level of mistrust have experienced a depletion of suitable staff and productivity as the workforce prefer to pursue a flexible option. It is important that the mind shift of acknowledging that the quality delivery of tasks should be the measure of productivity and not the actual time spent in the office.

The trend has evolved that an incumbent is no longer a specialist in one field all their life. With the ongoing development of new processes, technologies and systems in order to be successful there is a continual need for education and re-education. One big degree for a lifelong job at one corporation is being replaced by a culture of a repeatable cycle of learning then work, then learn again and work to sustain competitiveness in the labour market. It is fact that where in the past job hopping carried a considerable stigma, this is now more than ever becoming the norm.

In days gone by, the evidence of consistent job hopping on an applicant's resume hinted that in all likelihood presented a negative perception that the candidate probably had a people issue and did not get on with others, could not hold down a job, was disloyal and could not commit to a long term relationship.

The reality is that the opposite is becoming the actuality especially with regard to advancing through a continual learning and relearning process and the new job hopping millennia's are now perceived to possess a higher learning curve, perform better and deliver above expectations as they pursue the drive to make a favourable impression and assert themselves in a shorter time period with each employer.

Because such employees are continually challenging themselves outside their comfort zones they are typically over achievers who deliver a significant contribution to the bottom line which stands them in good stead before they move on to new opportunities every two to four years. It is believed that the learning curve tends to flatten after three years so in fact regular job hopping has become crucial to ensure a stable career growth.

It nevertheless can remain a concern for companies as there is a continual requirement to invest in new staff but the upside is that the rapid growth of the organisation and the worry of the loss of intellectual property to competitors is less threatening because the swift change makes the impact of the loss of such intellectual assets soon to be outdated.

The world is also seeing an exponential growth of entrepreneurs who with their specialised knowledge, offer their services on a short term basis simply by working as freelancers or contractors. With a wide-ranging exposure they enhance their skills and are thereby able to raise their rates or acquire additional freelancers to assist them and consequently grow their personal wealth.

Preparation of a Scenario Plan

Scenario planning can be defined as the blending of the known and unknown into a consistent future point of view. All our knowledge that we have is about the past, most of which can be described as we don't know what we don't know, a smaller percentage is knowing what it is that we don't know, and the smallest percentage is being aware of what it is that we actually do know. The conclusion is therefore the knowledge that is required in order to make good decisions is mostly beyond our comprehension.

Coupled to the knowledge base, the different types of futures can be categorised into "possible" or that which might happen based on future knowledge, that which is "plausible" which is what could happen and therefore depends on current knowledge, that what is "probable" based on current trends and lastly that which is "preferable" which is what we want to happen based on value judgments.

The proportionate levels of knowledge inputted into the different types of future

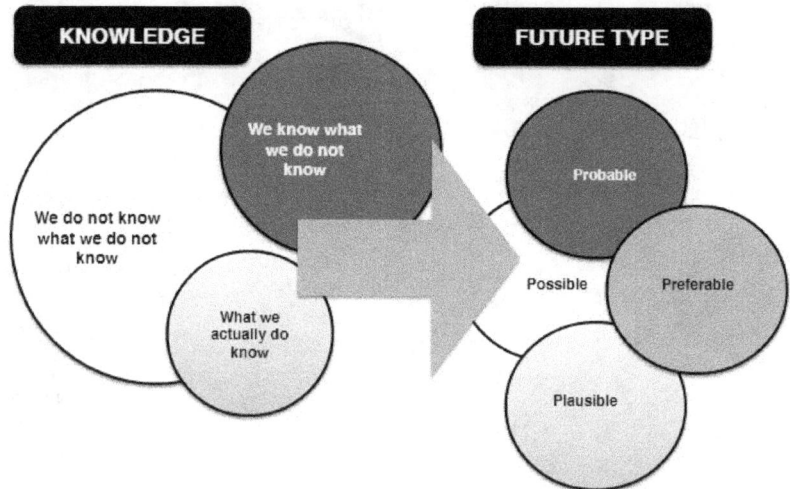

Scenarios can be described as possible views of the world in a narrative or story form which enables better informed forward decisions being able to be made which is likely to assist in the formulation of a successful strategy. It should be noted that scenarios do not predict the future but rather highlight those drivers that are most likely to influence the future and form part of the strategic management toolbox which consists of traditional methods which focus on the past while scenario planning tools focus on the future. By combining both the past and future the strategic thinking process is therefore stronger and enables better responsiveness, improved flexibility as well as generates a competitive advantage

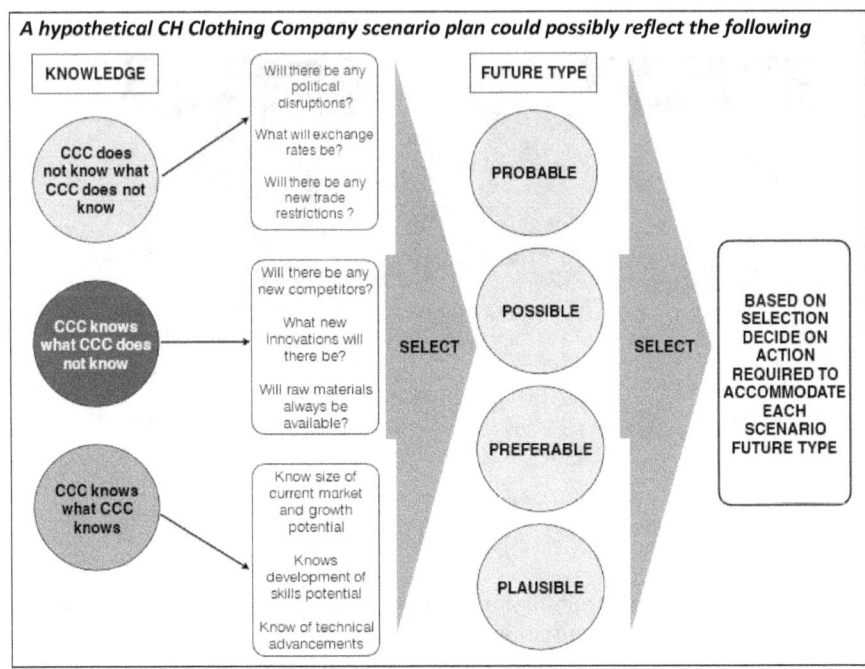

The creation of such scenarios follow a simple structured sequence of events where conscious long term judgments such as the identification of the major influences and factors within varying situations can bring about significant changes to the way business is done and deliver a diversity of results. Scenarios can be created through the grouping of complimentary influences into a framework of a number of "what if" situations. The number of these may then be reduced to an amount through amalgamation or elimination to end up with a manageable quantity of scenarios which would possibly have the greatest effect should they occur.

Selection of key drivers

After both an internal and external environmental scan is done, the consequence is the identification the key factors or subjects which may well decide the future nature of the environment in which the organisation will be operating. These forces will form the pillars of the areas which need to be examined and the specific definition of those drivers that will form the base of the different scenarios. Once the important topics are acknowledged, they are used to create scenarios which deliver alternative outcomes and should include the important predictable as well as the unknown outcomes. Typical examples of such drivers are those that represent the social, economic, technological, environmental, globalisation and political aspects.

The environmental scan will include an internal analysis of the company in terms of the strengths and weaknesses as well as an external scrutiny of the threats and opportunities which may or may not exist. Part of the scan will include an exploration of the industry that the business operates within. This will include the examination of the barriers that exist to enter the industry, the existing supplier infra-structure, customer base and evidence of substitution products as well as the rivalry intensity that is present amongst the participants.

After assessing the environmental scan, the firm will match those strengths they possess to their benefit and address the weaknesses as well as acknowledge the threats to the possible opportunities that may exist.

The macroeconomic environment factors also need to be taken into consideration, sometimes referred to as the PEST analysis (which is the acronym for political, economic, social and technological) that will impact on the firms operations.

Political factors include government regulations and legal issues under which the company must operate such as tax policy, employment laws and regulations, environment boundaries that may exist, trade restrictions and tariff structures as well as the overall political stability.

Economic facets that will influence the scenario planning process will be the economic growth, interest rates, inflation and exchange rates.

Social factors such as demographic and cultural aspects in the macroeconomic environment which will affect the customer needs and market penetration are typically health consciousness, population growth, the spread of age distribution and attitude to careers.

Technological factors such as automation, research and development will have significant impacts on production efficiencies and the extent that tasks need to be outsourced.

The hypothetical CH Clothing Company key drivers and factors identified during an environmental scan is illustrated below

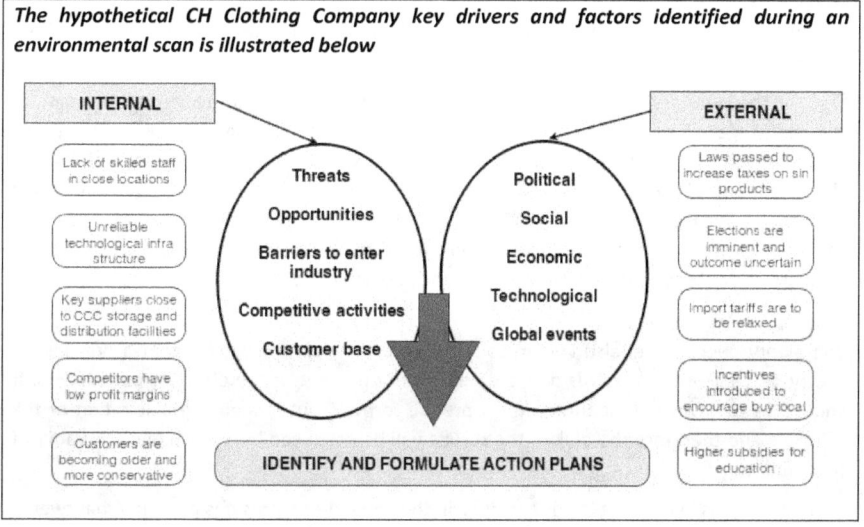

Brainstorming

Before we proceed any further it is valuable to describe a simple brainstorming process.

There are many techniques of brainstorming, some of which are more sophisticated than others. A very popular, basic and easy to use methodology, although it may be slower than other processes, is through the use of common sticky notelets.

All that is required is an isolated room with a clear wall and maybe a flip chart to list comments and park some issues for later discussion. The number of participants should not be too few but also not too large. In most cases the ideal quantity should be no more than fifteen which is a controllable amount that normally can be comfortably managed by the facilitator.

Prior to the commencement of the session the key drivers or pillars which were identified in the environmental analysis stage must be prominently indicated as the headings under which the sticky notelets will be randomly stuck on the wall which have the advantage that they can be removed or relocated as discussion progresses.

As is the case with the majority of brainstorming sessions, the generation of ideas invariably stimulate the creation of others which are pasted on the wall and the participants can move the posts around the wall under the designated headings as they wish. The process is relatively user friendly and therefore it is also easy for newcomers to grasp the concept and enjoy participating.

The illustrated example below assumes that the key drivers that will serve as the headings on the clear wall have been defined as political, social, technological, economic and environment.

The participants are then able to actively write their ideas on the notelets and paste them under the relevant heading.

Once all the ideas are exhausted and are evident on the wall under the appropriate headings the next stage will be to identify those that are important versus those that are not in terms of their levels of impact and uncertainty on the future. In order that this is done effectively the application of the eighty twenty rule is critical so that only those factors which are most relevant are focused on. Just allowing a number of topics to be randomly selected in terms of their perceived importance often results in those topics which are purely of interest being selected as opposed to those that are prioritised according to the commercial significance.

The eighty twenty rule

The eighty twenty rule, also known as the Pareto principle, recognises that a principle of eighty percent of the result is delivered by twenty percent of the effort or participants. It should be recognised that this is not a precise formula but is more an illustration of the principle and therefore the bulk of the results will be produced by a much lower number of participants.

Prime examples in retailing is, for example, in the context of stores it is probable that twenty percent of the stores deliver eighty percent of the sales and deserve the proportionate dedication of energy and focus, as does the thick middle sizes such as medium and large and therefore should always be in stock. Core base colours such as white, black, naturals and greys also contribute largely to the sales and should always be evident in volume. It is clear that certain styling features will likewise guarantee the bulk of sales and should be finalised first and certain peak trading periods such as holidays or special events will contribute largely to the total seasonal sales and must be managed very carefully in terms of production planning and delivery scheduling.

Once the important topics are identified, the use of them to create scenarios which deliver alternative outcomes should include the important predictable inferences as well as fictional conclusions.

The next step is to integrate these key influences and thereby create a framework or scenario matrix. The linking of some of the influences can take place where the characteristic of one factor may be relevant to another while, on the other hand this may not always be the case. The brainstorm participants therefore arrange the elements into groups that have relevance and make some sense. The amount of groups that emerge will be dependent on the number of elements available to contemplate. While this process is in progress it is possible that new groupings may be added while others could be removed. As these clusters of elements materialise, the creation of the mini scenarios may be linked together based on their similarities or mutual influence and eventually a process of rationalising and absorption can take place to condense the mini scenarios into two or three core scenarios. All of the above will entail extensive debate before common ground is met in order to agree the fundamental insights into what the really imperative issues are applicable to the organisation. Once this stage is achieved, because of the intimate understanding of the participants that has developed, it will be almost instinctive without any reference to any formal report to know how to cope with potential issues should and when they materialise.

Presentation of scenarios

The final two or three scenarios that are constructed need to be written up in a formal format to serve as a consistent guideline for team leaders to base their strategy on. The report will in essence be more qualitative rather than be peppered with intense detail although reference may be made to tabular work and diagrams but in whatever emphasis this happens, the report needs to remain factual.

An example of the simplistic building of a scenario plan using the process described above is depicted below

Key headings and notelets pasted below on the clear wall with the annotation of importance of each comment in terms of impact relative to uncertainty is depicted as follows

POLITICAL	SOCIAL	TECHNOLOGICAL	ECONOMIC	ENVIRONMENT
Influence of global governments	Increasing population	Increasing reliance on technology	Declining trade of traditional commodities	Increasing acceptance of environment awareness
1 Li/Hu	2 Mi/Mu	3 Hi/Lu	4 Li/Mu	5 Mi/Mu
Influence of dominant world leaders	Aged more economically active	Improved health environment through better technologies	Globalisation	Continued degradation of natural environment
6 Mi/Mu	7 Hi/Lu	8 Mi/Mu	9 Mi/Lu	10 Hi/Lu
Global conflict	Cultural transformation through globalization, immigration and technology	Newer and cleaner renewable energy resources now viable	New technologies creating channels for empoyment	Declining water quality
11 Hi/Mu	12 Li/Mu	13 Hi/Hu	14 Li/Hu	15 Hi/Mu
Terrorism	Increased life expectancy and quality health support	Increasing technological devices making shopping easier	Evolution of single global currency	Declining air quality and increased energy consumption
16 Hi/Hu	17 Mi/Lu	18 Li/Hu	19 Mi/Hu	20 Mi/Hu
Influence of key election results	Rural areas being developed increased urbanisation	Combination of technologies to make on line trading become economically efficient	Traditional employment approach creating unemployment	Impact of global climate change
21 Li/Lu	22 Li/Lu	23 Mi/Lu	24 Li/Lu	25 Li/Mu
Influence of non government organisations				
26 Li/Hu				

Uncertainty

Low (Lu) – very that activity will happen in the way that we expect

High (Hu) – no certainty as to what will happen

Med (Mu) – somewhere in between

Impact

Low (Li) – effect of activity will deliver low results

High (Hi) – effect of activity will deliver high results

Med (Mi) – somewhere in between

A Scattergram below illustrates according to the corresponding shapes the relative significance of impact and uncertainty of each comment

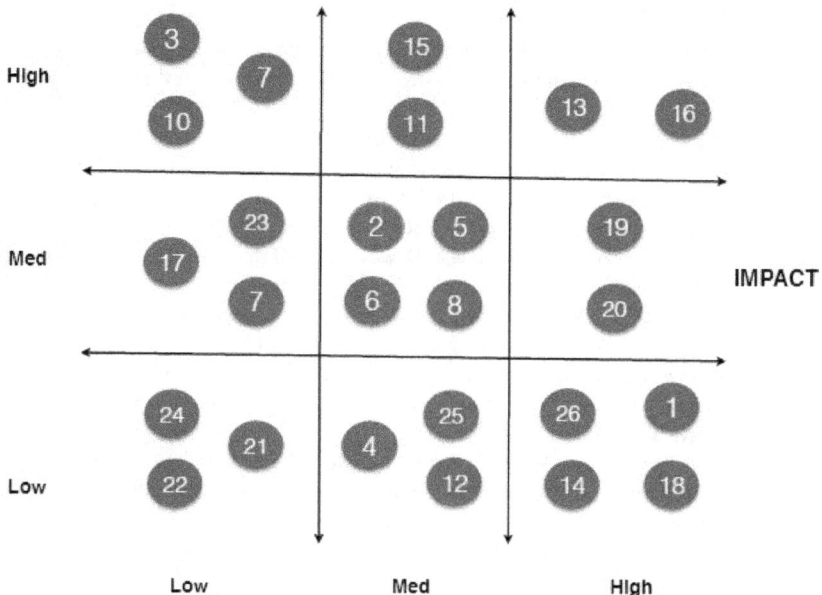

UNCERTAINTY

The two highest uncertainty and highest impact critical external factors (right top of the matrix) which will be selected according to our model will be

-   Terrorism
-   New and cleaner renewable energy resources which are now economically viable

The three most critical internal factors in terms of impact and uncertainty which will be selected are

-   Increase in market penetration through innovative and technological methodologies
-   Availability of safe retail space
-   Supplier management and sustainability

In the scenario workshop the participants will need to consider the world of the future taking into account the external and internal factors and the influence they will have in creating the environment in which trade will take place.

During the process of imagining the world of the future it is essential that participants are not influenced by personal opinions such as not believing it possible, mistrust and relying on intuition but should rather focus on the plausibility perspective. By way of illustration the drafting of the scenario of the future period must be therefore be done taking into account the following types of points

-   What will the world be like going forward? To do this take into account the events that brought change to where you are now and project those events that will influence the world going forward.
-   In building a picture of a future world consideration should be given to the effect of current indicators are not necessarily a foregone conclusion should they change significantly. As an example, if the borrowing interests increase, the growth of the economy will probably be undermined and consequently the currency in relation to other currencies will be worth less. However even if the interest rates are conversely reduced unless the domestic demand for product is strong enough, the currency could still deteriorate. The possibility of exporting more product, or attracting more tourism will have a positive influence on growth as will attracting foreign investors. Commodity prices will also change the landscape dramatically such as a weak oil price will enable cheaper costs but it may not be weak but is gaining strength so in this case will have the reverse effect.
-   Will your organisation exist in this new world going forward? What would you look like? Are you going to be global? Will you be virtual or physical? What will your customer look like? What will your organisational structure look like?
-   The drafting and presentation of the scenario does not have to be off the wall but above all should be creative.

The main uses of scenarios is to provide a common language for ongoing forward discussions, assess the risks involved when taking specific decisions, assist in the evaluation of current strategies as well as in the development of new strategies.

Scenarios provide clues as to what the strategic drivers of the future might be, how they may interact and in what way they may affect the organisation. The identification of robust strategies that will be able to survive future scenarios is key and are able to assist in detecting early warning indicators to know what to do in the occurrence of such events, some of which may be catastrophic beyond control, wide in scope and rapidly moving. Examples of such events could be a stock market collapse, a terrorist attack or disrupted water and electricity supply.

One certain conclusion about change is that change will happen. The skill is, through scenario planning is to identify in what way organisations will change. Examples of how they are likely to change could be such as from an autocratic environment to an empowerment one, from a structured life to an unstructured life, from a volume based production base to a need for speed to market base, from high predictability based on historical trends to a world of uncertainty, from slow change to rapid change and ambiguity, from reliance on processes to reliance on people, from structured hierarchical organisations to alliances and coalitions, from avoiding risk to managing risk.

The final message to take note of is that the traditional strategic planning processes are no longer sufficient on their own but need the support of well thought out perceptions of the future.

Below is a simplified example of a hypothetical CH Clothing Company scenario view which under the key driver groupings certain events are listed and tagged in terms of the levels of certainty that are prevalent. Added to this, comment is made as to the form and impact that these events may take.

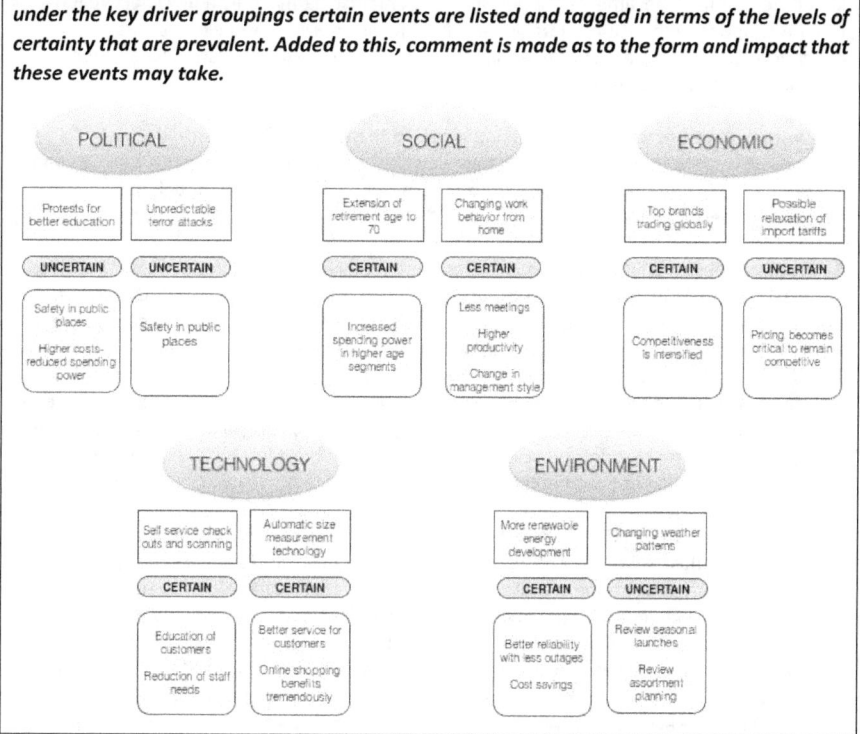

During some of my research, I came across an article written by Robert M. Goldman MD, PhD, DO, FAASP that had such an impact on me in terms of the illustration as to what has happened and what potentially can happen in our world, I felt it best be presented verbatim to maximise the message.

FUTURE PREDICTIONS

In 1998, Kodak had 170,000 employees and sold 85% of all photo paper worldwide. Within just a few years, their business model disappeared and they went bankrupt. What happened to Kodak will happen in a lot of industries in the next 10 years - and most people don't see it coming. Did you think in 1998 that 3 years later you would never take pictures on paper film again? Yet digital cameras were invented in 1975. The first ones only had 10,000 pixels, but followed Moore's law. So as with all exponential technologies, it was a disappointment for a long time, before it became way superior and got mainstream in only a few short years. It will now happen with Artificial Intelligence, health, autonomous and electric cars, education, 3D printing, agriculture and jobs. Welcome to the 4th Industrial Revolution. Welcome to the Exponential Age.

Software will disrupt most traditional industries in the next 5-10 years.
Uber is just a software tool, they don't own any cars, and are now the biggest taxi company in the world. Airbnb is now the biggest hotel company in the world, although they don't own any properties.

Artificial Intelligence: Computers become exponentially better in understanding the world. This year, a computer beat the best Go player in the world, 10 years earlier than expected. In the US, young lawyers already don't get jobs. Because of IBM Watson, you can get legal advice (so far for more or less basic stuff) within seconds, with 90% accuracy compared with 70% accuracy when done by humans. So if you study law, stop immediately. There will be 90% fewer lawyers in the future, only specialists will remain. Watson already helps nurses diagnosing cancer, 4 time more accurate than human nurses. Facebook now has a pattern recognition software that can recognize faces better than humans. By 2030, computers will become more intelligent than humans.

Autonomous Cars: In 2018 the first self-driving cars will appear for the public. Around 2020, the complete industry will start to be disrupted. You don't want to own a car anymore. You will call a car with your phone, it will show up at your location and drive you to your destination. You will not need to park it, you only pay for the driven distance and can be productive while driving. Our kids will never get a driver's license and will never own a car. It will change the cities, because we will need 90-95% fewer cars for that. We can transform former parking space into parks. 1.2 million people die each year in car accidents worldwide. We now have one accident every 100,000 km, with autonomous driving that will drop to one accident in 10 million km. That will save a million lives each year.

Most car companies may become bankrupt. Traditional car companies try the evolutionary approach and just build a better car, while tech companies (Tesla, Apple, Google) will do the revolutionary approach and build a computer on wheels. I spoke to a lot of engineers from Volkswagen and Audi; they are completely terrified of Tesla.

Insurance Companies will have massive trouble because without accidents, the insurance will become 100x cheaper. Their car insurance business model will disappear.

Real estate will change. Because if you can work while you commute, people will move further away to live in a more beautiful neighbourhood.

Electric cars won't become mainstream until 2020. Cities will be less noisy because all cars will run on electric. Electricity will become incredibly cheap and clean: Solar production has been on an exponential curve for 30 years, but you can only now see the impact. Last year, more solar energy was installed worldwide than fossil. The price for solar will drop so much that all coal companies will be out of business by 2025.

With cheap electricity comes cheap and abundant water. Desalination now only needs 2kWh per cubic meter. We don't have scarce water in most places, we only have scarce drinking water. Imagine what will be possible if anyone can have as much clean water as he wants, for nearly no cost.

Health: There will be companies that will build a medical device (called the "Tricorder" from Star Trek) that works with your phone, which takes your retina scan, your blood sample and you breathe into it. It then analyses 54 biomarkers that will identify nearly any disease. It will be cheap, so in a few years everyone on this planet will have access to world class medicine, nearly for free.

3D printing: The price of the cheapest 3D printer came down from $18,000 to $400 within 10 years. In the same time, it became 100 times faster. All major shoe companies started 3D printing shoes. Spare airplane parts are already 3D printed in remote airports. The space station now has a printer that eliminates the need for the large number of spare parts they used to have in the past.

At the end of this year, new smart phones will have 3D scanning possibilities. You can then 3D scan your feet and print your perfect shoe at home. In China, they already 3D printed a complete 6-storey office building. By 2027, 10% of everything that's being produced will be 3D printed.

Business Opportunities: If you think of a niche you want to go in, ask yourself: "in the future, do you think we will have that?" and if the answer is yes, how can you make that happen sooner? If it doesn't work with your phone, forget the idea. And any idea designed for success in the 20th century is doomed in to failure in the 21st century.

Work: 70-80% of jobs will disappear in the next 20 years. There will be a lot of new jobs, but it is not clear if there will be enough new jobs in such a small time.

Agriculture: There will be a $100 agricultural robot in the future. Farmers in 3rd world countries can then become managers of their field instead of working all days on their fields. Agroponics will need much less water. The first Petri dish produced veal is now available and will be cheaper than cow-produced veal in 2018. Right now, 30% of all agricultural surfaces is used for cows. Imagine if we don't need that space anymore. There are several startups that will bring insect protein to the market shortly. It contains more protein than meat. It will be labelled as "alternative protein source" (because most people still reject the idea of eating insects).

There is an app called "moodies" which can already tell in which mood you are. Until 2020 there will be apps that can tell by your facial expressions if you are lying. Imagine a political debate where it's being displayed when they are telling the truth and when not.

Bitcoin will become mainstream this year and might even become the default reserve currency.

Longevity: Right now, the average life span increases by 3 months per year. Four years ago, the life span used to be 79 years, now it's 80 years. The increase itself is increasing and by 2036, there will be more than one year increase per year. So we all might live for a long long time, probably way more than 100.

Education: The cheapest smart phones are already at $10 in Africa and Asia. Until 2020, 70% of all humans will own a smart phone. That means, everyone has the same access to world class education.

Robert M. Goldman MD, PhD, DO, FAASP
www.DrBobGoldman.com
World Chairman-International Medical Commission
Co-Founder & Chairman of the Board-A4M
Founder & Chairman-International Sports Hall of Fame
Co-Founder & Chairman-World Academy of Anti-Aging Medicine
President Emeritus-National Academy of Sports Medicine (NASM)
Chairman-U.S. Sports Academy's Board of Visitors

STRATEGIC PLANNING

The commencement of the process to draft and implement a strategic plan follows a set sequence of events that form the foundation of a blueprint that needs to be followed to develop a sustainable plan of action going forward.

The type of points that need to be addressed in the drafting of a plan is to know what the vision together with the corresponding mission is. The relevant customer and their desires specific to the retailer have to be intimately clear.

The strategy ought to be aimed specifically at them in order that the purpose and values of the business is linked by the strategy to the right customer and the other stakeholders. It is therefore important that the strategy is sustainable over the longer term through clear communication, that it directs the focus and effort and thereby energises and inspires people to consistently perform at optimal levels.

Competitors should be clearly identified as well as the factors that will influence both the customer and the competitors of the future. Added to this the competitors are becoming increasingly hostile in a global market which adds complexity bringing with it more challenges requiring additional thought to transform ideas into action in a much shorter space of time often with limited resources. It is therefore absolutely imperative that the retailer should know as much about their competitors as possible and should in fact construct a dossier on each of their foremost challengers. Knowing who the direct and indirect contenders are and how they are performing in the market place, what can be learnt from their operations, what their strengths and weaknesses are, how different they are, the frequency and what media is used to advertise as well as what pricing strategy is employed will assist in the intimate understanding of competitors.

There are two basic types of competitive advantage which are the cost factor whereby the product is the same or similar in form and function to competitors but is made available at a lower price. The second advantage is the difference in the form of added value the product possesses compared to other products on offer in the market. The strategic activities may include plans to create the competitive advantage in one way or the other through the processes as outlined below.

In the strategic planning process the weaknesses need to be emphasised in order to minimise risks, the strengths must to be continuously capitilised upon while at the same time the appreciation of any threats to the business which may hamper the progress has to be taken into account. With all these factors in mind the plan of appropriate operational activities must be formulated in such a way that they are aligned to the vision of the company and support the basis of the strategy.

A firm's strengths are its resources and capabilities to gain competitive advantage and typical of these are patents, reputable brands, reputation, cost advantages and access to effective distribution networks.

The absence of certain strengths can be interpreted as weaknesses and could include factors such as absence of patent protection, weak brands and lack of reputation, high cost structures and poor distribution channels.

The external environmental analysis may result in the identification of the emergence of opportunities for growth and profit as well as certain threats. Examples of opportunities could be the evolvement of new customer needs, development of new technologies, the relaxation of regulations and the possible removal of international trade barriers. The opposite of the opportunities could in turn be seen as the threats to the firm such as the shift away from the products by the customers, the emergence of substitute products, new regulations and the imposition of international trade barriers.

This dependable interpretation of the strategy will enable the planning of management activity that is used to set the priorities, focus energy and resources, strengthen the operational events while ensuring all the key stakeholders are aligned in such a way that the overall company strategic goals are achieved. A documented strategic plan is formulated which communicates the goals and the operational activities that are required to achieve them. Management of the plan must ensure that the processes are systematically coordinated and the resources and actions are aligned with the mission, vision and strategy throughout the organisation.

The framework and methodologies of managing the strategic plan broadly follow the same sequence of phases which are that the understanding of the external and internal environments is developed, the formulation of the strategy is documented, a corresponding operational plan of activities required to achieve the strategic goals is drafted and lastly, the evaluation and sustainability of the plan is managed and continually refined through performance measurement, communications and data reporting.

Diagrammatically the process cycle of strategic planning can be depicted as follows

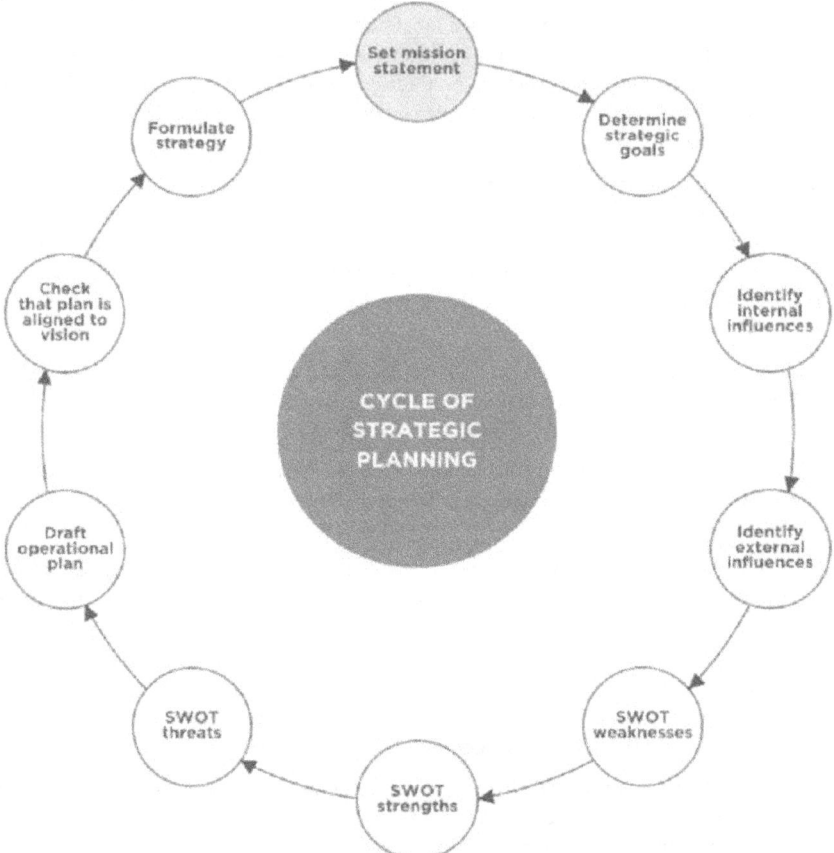

By way of illustration a hypothetical retailer has been formed which follows the creation of the strategy and the subsequent operational plan. In broad terms the business firstly documents its vision which describes the blue sky dream of becoming a preferred retailer which offers clothing that represents exceptional value, is up to date with current trends and is purposeful in both form and function.

The company has a mission to expertly fulfill the customers' needs transparently in such a way that they can be trusted and sustain a high level of integrity.

In order that this can be achieved adequately the set of goals need to be identified that are realistic, are able to be benchmarked and measured. In the simplistic model outlined below there are basically three goals that need to be focused on which are growing market penetration by one percent through the optimum use of media, expand real estate to cater for all regions and develop and implement tools of measurement of supplier performance to ensure the optimum delivery of product to maximise profit opportunities.

In order to remain focused it is imperative to identify where the strong points are such as a loyal customer base and trustworthy and reliable suppliers and constantly focus on protecting these qualities. On the other hand it should be acknowledged that they may well be behind the rest of the field in terms of technologically advanced competitors who are reaping the benefits of digital retail channels and should grasp the potential development of such vehicles as a wonderful opportunity to acquire similar benefits that the competitors do.

A simplistic example of the strategic plan of the hypothetical CH Clothing Company can be as outlined below

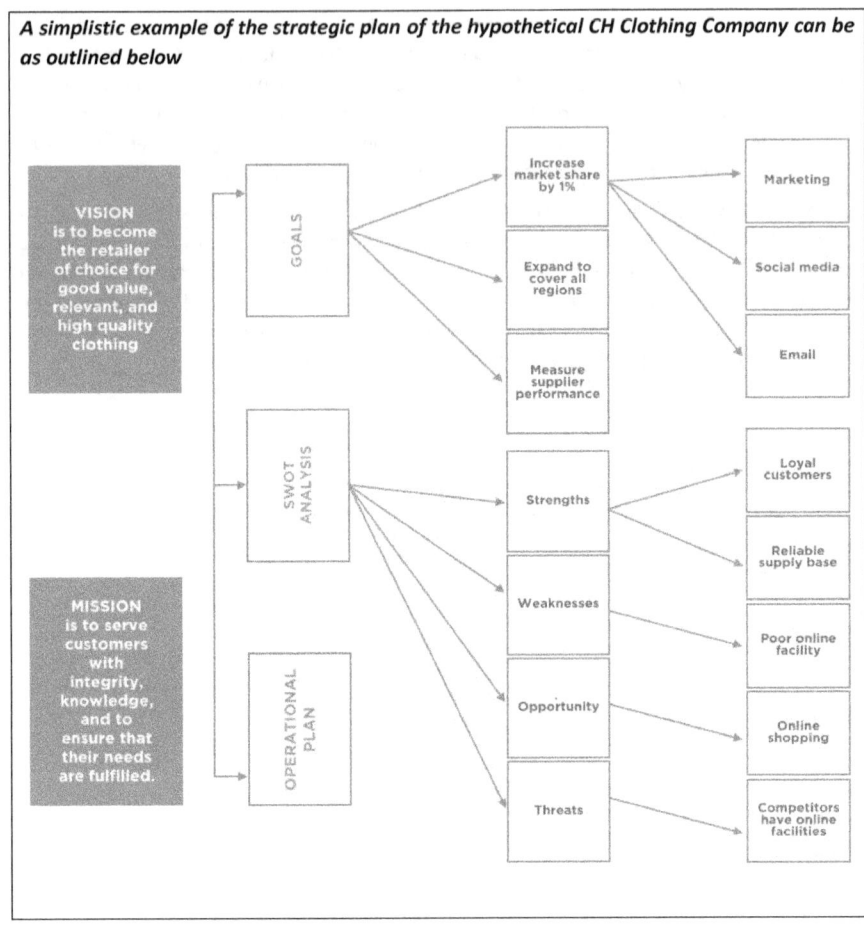

As has been stated, the strategic thinking delivers what is desired to be delivered while the operational aspect provides guidance as to how the objectives are going to materialise. The example of the hypothetical retailer who wishes to be a retailer of choice may wish to use the advantage derived from loyalty programmes which could be in the form of discount coupons, the publication of own brand magazines and derive the benefit of sophisticated analysis of the consumer data base to gain better understanding of their customer profile.

The desired sales outlet expansion will have to be achieved through opening of new stores, the remodeling and enlargement of existing stores, expansion of newer formats with the exploitation of those categories which offer the most potential opportunities and the development of an on line sales channel all of which will demand additional location sites, design and IT resources.

The effective measurement of supplier efficiencies will require measurement tools and a reporting infrastructure which will preferably be available on line and provide for a system of penalties for underperformers and incentives for those suppliers who exceed expectation.

The corresponding operational plan of the hypothetical CH Clothing Company strategic plan above will therefore possibly look like

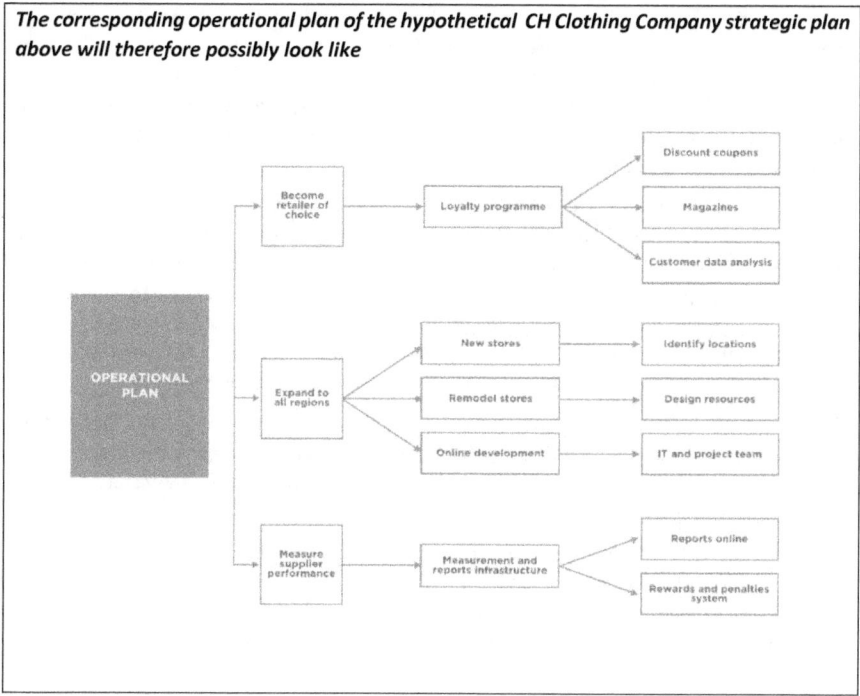

The consequences of poorly thought out strategies can be devastating. There are many examples of once extremely successful chains whose buildings that were landmarks are today parking garages. Retailers who have a tendency to doubt outlooks are often displayed through the rear view mirror images which tells us from where we have come has always worked and the subsequent question asked is more often than not "if it is not broken why change?"

The very successful, intelligent captains of such firms often succumb to the destruction of once successful business for a number of reasons. The fear of change is more often than not the cause because the potential is not viewed as an opportunity but rather seen as a risk. When there is a trend being followed by competitors or new entries to the market an air of arrogance takes hold and the dogged belief is upheld that the current trading philosophies which are set in concrete will withstand the onslaught and any other unfamiliar options are doomed to failure.

Taking the importance of new strategic objectives seriously is seen at times as just another routine task on the calendar which needs to be completed but in reality the focus quickly apathetically returns to complete the current responsibilities as before to sustain the operation.

The lack of the leaders who see the big picture and miss out on the benefits in total can be extremely damaging. In their place is only those who resolutely continue the practice of working within their own relevant areas of control and comfort zones and do not consequently contribute to the achievement of an overall vision. Invariably it is the personal objective that dominates which is one of self-preservation as is reflected in the view that as long as their area has performed within the required parameters any failures that may arise cannot be attributed to them.

Similarly some organisations, characteristically those that are family driven or are by nature very staid with autocratic leadership frequently lack imagination to foresee change or are reluctant to "think out of the box" and consequently there is an unwillingness to innovate. When such an approach is challenged it is often met with obstinacy to hold on to what's more certain, defined and secure which is in the present. The effect is that the argument for change is often justified by making the situation sound less critical than it really is and is stereotypically confirmed by erroneous comparisons to other existing case studies.

The success of retailers is frequently measured by the scale of operations and share value rather than by the product quality, shopping experience and resultantly the usage of the phrase "customer service" becomes trite and is nothing but just a throw away statement.

In many circumstances operations were in recent years dominated by the availability of easy credit at stores where the needs of the customer were broadly projected and the product was bought in high volumes across a limited number of categories to lever better prices from vendors. The driving force was to sell them as quickly as possible using mediocre service. Consequently innovation and revitalised selling formats were almost totally stagnant for many years.

The reality is that the consumer has become conscious to this fact and it does not inspire them any longer to remain loyal to a specific brand but rather to source out the retailers who are sincere in their messages, offer service of difference whereby the customers can truly appreciate a better experience. Much of the success of the newer revolutionary retailers is that they have identities that the consumer associate with which may be cultural such as an eastern philosophies, sporting associations with an emphasis on lifestyle and role models where the markets are not dependent on mass and discount but on meaning and have become communities in themselves.

The point needs to be made that it takes some bold mind shifts when the writing is on the wall that failure is imminent and the need to manage the way out of the situation calls for outside interventions, new strategies and tactics and respect in order to emerge on the other side of the storm successfully.

There are some key philosophies that need to be applied to rescue struggling businesses and it is only through embracing these that will possibly provide the essential lifeline. Innovation or evaporate is an ultimatum that cannot be ignored because unless there is some form of reinvention it is without doubt that through doing the same thing over and over again it is guaranteed that oblivion will be the consequence. Knowing your market and their expectations is critical and working within these parameters is paramount and venturing outside these boundaries is likely to lead to confusion and mistrust. Often success can in itself be a stumbling block as it leads to a sense of euphoria and invincibility with an element of complacency. This is a reason why great leaders will continually be questioning as to what is next. Updated systems are key to keeping up with the pack and so often the neglect to adopt newer applications results in calamity and often enforces urgent catch up programmes to remain relevant in the market place. Lastly but without doubt the most important point is to remember that the customer is king and if an attitude is adopted that they can be dictated to often leads to rejection unless focus is fully maintained on their changing desires, requirements and needs.

STRATEGIC STAKEHOLDERS

In a clothing retail environment the typical individual stakeholder areas need to focus on their independent strategies for a specific period of time that together must be aligned to meet the overall company strategic objectives. It is therefore imperative that the different areas are scrutinized and activities are adapted to ensure that this objective is achieved.

Illustratively the various pertinent strategic focus areas are depicted as follows

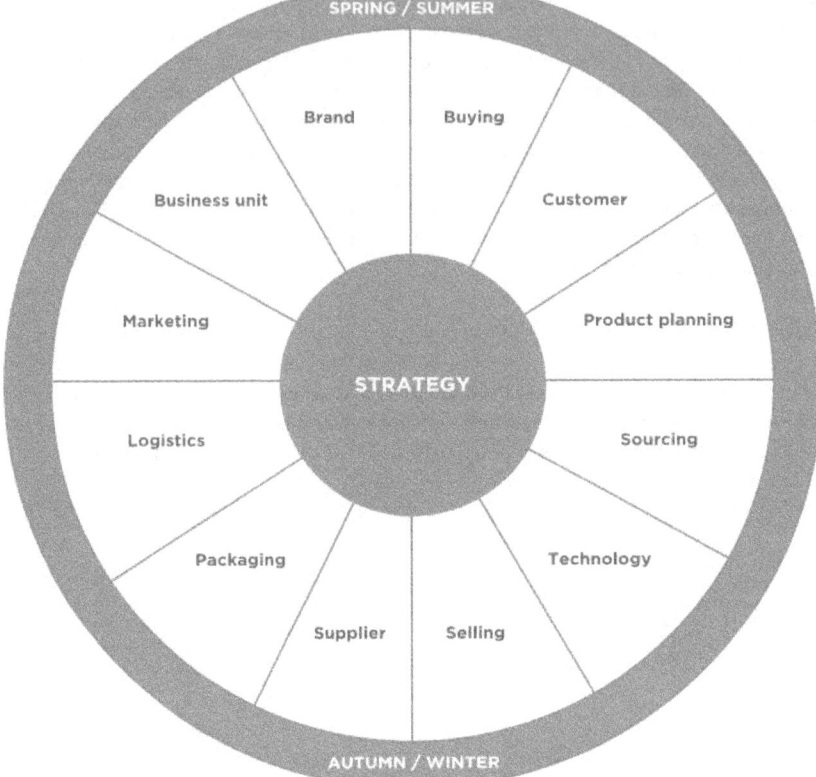

Business unit strategy

The leaders representing each of the key areas will construct the overall company strategy more often than not on an annual basis with interim updates for a specific period as well as for an extended future time thereafter up to as much as three years.

The corporate strategy development and co-ordination is concerned with the definition of the issues that are corporate responsibilities. These may be in the form of the definition of the overall goals as well as the way in which the key stakeholders are integrated and managed.

Fundamental for the company's success is the need to nurture an environment wherein all employees are able to conduct their business in pleasant conditions with fair remuneration enjoying personal recognition and job security. Coupled to this will be the investment of finances across the various components and the development of synergies by the sharing and co-ordination of resources and staff across the different units across the company. The way the units will be governed, either in a centralised or decentralised format will influence the effectiveness of the sharing of resources and staff and therefore this should be considered very carefully in the formulation of the corporate strategy.

Factors which that need to be taken into account in the construction of the overall strategy will be the historical trading performance, current business trends, competitor activity, customer demographics, the growth of new emerging markets, economic trends like increasing fuel prices and interest rates, and evolving trends which can translate into new business opportunities, as is the case of procuring better value goods from off shore suppliers and initiatives like the exponential increase of on line shopping.

Using internal and external research with the evaluation of past performance will determine the budget targets, key performance goals and market penetration potential.

Out of the strategic workshop including the identification and management of the synergies between the key operating areas a corporate operational plan will be developed and disseminated to the relevant business areas to give guidance in the construction of their own individual strategies to ensure that the overall objectives of the company are met. This would include the need for shifts in retail, financial, marketing, information technology, real estate strategies, the sourcing of suppliers, logistical processes and provide individual operational plans that will ensure that the modifications and new initiatives are all catered for. Examples of changes may include action to penetrate new or better serve customer profiles, expand retail channels such as on line, to open new stores in new locations, implement innovative systems and reduce lead times. Fresh initiatives may be in the form of adding new product types, acquisitions, enhancing logistical operations and implement an innovative variation of loyalty programmes.

The hypothetical CH Clothing Company diagrammatic business unit strategy in terms of the development of a corporate operational plan that will give guidance to the critical key areas would probably resemble a format with action plans to ensure new initiatives will be catered for as follows

STRATEGIC KEY AREAS	ACTION REQUIRED	OBJECTIVE
REAL ESTATE	Identify sites for new locations, refurbish older 'tired' stores and investigate enhancement of on line facilities	Provide inspiring and comfortable shopping environment to maximize sales through an 8.0% increase in turnover
SUPPLIER SOURCING	Investigate reliable suppliers with quick manufacturing response	Have fast availability of quality on time merchandise close to market for an increase of 2.0% in delivery efficiency
LOGISTICS	Consider extra regional warehousing and distribution centre close to market	Reduction of average delivery lead times by at least three days
FINANCIALS	Re-negotiate payment terms and quantity discounts with incentive performance rewards	Contribute to the maximization of profit from a financial perspective by a selling margin increase of 0.25%
MARKETING	Introduce innovative loyalty program and increased use of social media initiatives	Increase market penetration by at least 0.5%
INFORMATION TECHNOLOGY	Identify, purchase and develop an integrated planning tool to maximize reliability and integrity of data	Will improve accuracy, speed and integrity to increase profitability by at least 1.0%
PRODUCT	Review assortment of product selection to ensure a balanced, co-ordinated product offer continuously	Provide a wanted selection of merchandise in continuity which will improve turnover by 3.0%

Brand strategy

A considered view of the external and internal retail landscape has to be documented and understood. In order to enable this, team members in the buying groups, marketing, sourcing, technology, packaging, the store's visual team and designers will workshop the information gathered from past sales performance and take on board lessons learnt from the previous season, market share information, loyalty programme data analysis together with trends evident at global trade shows, catwalks, other retailers, suppliers, internet and social media.

From a planning perspective, the analysis of trade at the conclusion of the season which must include space productivity analysis and the modification of the merchandising targets need to be accounted for in terms of the impact on the brand. Typical examples of such aspects would be the effect on the customer profiles and the market penetration opportunities that arise, the open to buy reserve quantities to enable flexibility and impact on stock management and other key performance indicators which may need to be modified.

The task that is undertaken is the formulation of the direction of emerging trends in designs, core fabrics, colours, technical innovation and packaging, marketing communication as well as the highlighting of key global customer and lifestyle trends. These developments can be applied to the future season together with the identification of potential customer penetration opportunities which is vital in the input for the construction of the group buying strategies.

Service is very much a critical component of branding particularly where the retailer is own brand active and that if unsatisfactory service persists it will be unlikely that the operational expectations will be delivered. Experience shows again and again that excellent customer service lowers customer attrition rates, fosters positive messaging via word of mouth and with this comes significant increases in sales.

Some of the key ways that retailers can make their customers feel more valued include the following. It is paramount to always say thank you whether it is verbally or in the form of a token it must be sincere. In order to boost your brand reputation. In instances where disputes may arise it is critical to give the customer the benefit of the doubt and work with the customer to resolve their concerns and offer great service in the process. Satisfying the customer is everyone's priority, including the executive leadership and understand that the company needs the customer more than the customer needs the company.

It is a proven fact that across a number of countries where there is an offer of digital service options such as e-mails, SMS, internet sites or social media vehicles nearly eighty percent of customers prefer the direct contact with humans either directly or via the telephone as the preferred channel of customer service when engaging with brands or service providers. This is in spite of the fact that consumers are becoming increasingly familiar with digital channels.

The positioning of the brand in the market place amongst all other competitors is determined by the attributes that make up the character of the product which helps to evaluate the product positioning in relation to other retailers and assist in ensuring that the right emphasis is achieved in order to maximise opportunities. It is critical that fashion retailers have a clear perception as to where they are positioned otherwise customers will become confused and will drift away to alternative contenders who give a clearer message as to what they stand for through the distinctive branding that identifies them.

The market positioning provides the customer with an awareness of the borders wherein the products fall and decree what they would expect to buy from the retailer. A prime example would be where a high fashion retailer introduces a traditional and conservative range of merchandise which would then send out a message that there is an older profile customer shopping in the store. It is therefore important that when a retailer consciously makes changes whether it be style, price or new ranges to reposition themselves that this intention is clearly communicated through appropriate marketing channels to the customer. Failure to do so effectively could result in them running the risk of significant write downs.

In terms of the advertising of your product, it should be noted that advertising itself does not physically sell the product but rather the idea and basis a scenario that fulfils the customer needs in order to persuade them to buy. This objective makes the realistic, honest descriptive copy and illustrative content of prime importance.

It is also important to have a good logo that will establish the brand identity, enhance the customer loyalty and can influence purchase decisions. In order to achieve this, there are some important guidelines that should be adhered to during the creation of a logo. For a start the colour of the logo ought to convey the right mood or message to your target audience. For example, studies in the psychology of colour deduce that green is associated with nature and life while blue expresses community and trust while black is linked to elegance. It is therefore paramount to choose a colour that reflects the company personality. The logo has to be versatile in that it must be adaptable for all vehicles from billboards to business card and brochures and should look equally good in both multi-colour and black and white formats. The typography also reflects the personality of the brand and needs to be accepted by the right target market, for example, script typefaces project young and fun images while serif typefaces convey a sense of dignity and power. The logo must be unique in that it stands out from the competition while at the same time be able to stand the test of time.

The positioning of the brand in the market is best communicated to the customer by building a marketing mix matrix which will be perceived and understood by the customers and will also facilitate benchmarks as points of reference for the retailer to compare with competitors. Distinctive branding is achieved through precise marketing, commendable public relations, a sound corporate identity and consistent messaging and image building through consistent advertising.

In the illustration below the attributes are positioned on the varying extreme scales of fashionability and value in the market and serves as a check for the retailer to ensure that they are best catering for their target customer profile by ticking off the qualities that suitably represent their products

The brand can be described as the personality of the retailer.

A brand positioning model in the market can be illustrated as follows

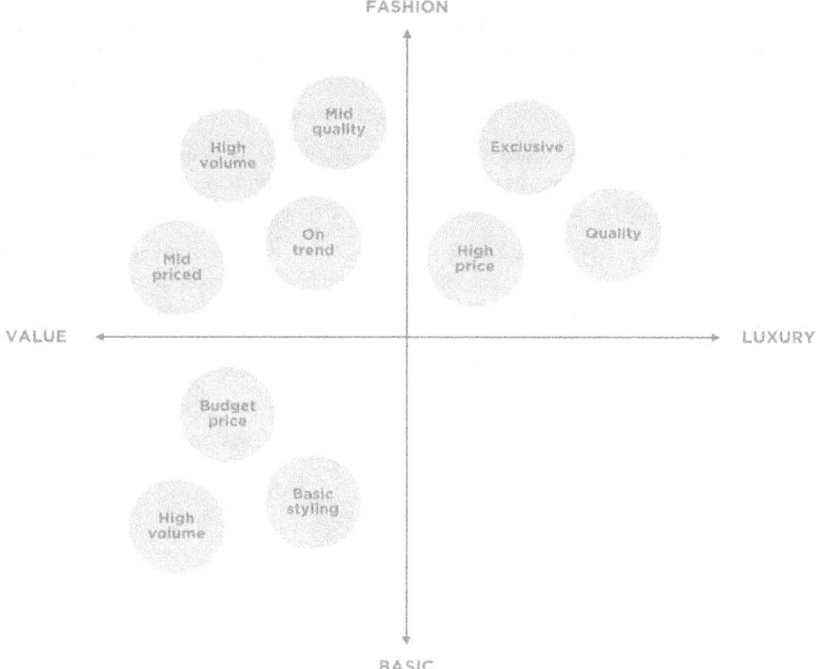

Buying group strategy

The buying group is a strategic business unit which as a profit centre can be planned independently and are less about the co-ordination of operating units but are more focused on the development and sustaining a competitive advantage for the goods that are put on offer for sale.

The formulation of the strategy is therefore more focussed on the positioning of the group against the rivals, the anticipation of the changes in demand and innovating competitive advantages such as the creation of new distribution channels or pursuing new technologies, improving product differentiation and streamlining the manufacturing processes.

Utilising the total company strategy as an input into the buying group strategy for the season will ensure that they stay aligned to the higher level objectives. The similar focus points will be considered and interpreted as they pertain to the specific buying group. Customer and trend direction must be adapted accordingly and the financial budgets, product mix of the group will need to be reviewed as a result. For a six month season period which may be split into sub seasonal periods, in other words, the six month winter period may well consist of a transitional three month autumn period and a high season winter time.

The trading performance and lessons learnt from the previous season as well as the customer penetration opportunities together with the competitor activity and economic landscape has to be assessed. Adjustments to the targets of the key performance measurements may have to be made to align the strategy. The customer profile relating to lifestyle and the trend forecast for the specific target market pertaining to the specific business unit will be analysed as will the financial budgets and import versus local procurement.

The strategy has to be tested against the other supporting stakeholders such as logistics, marketing, IT initiatives, human resources, trend sourcing plans and packaging revisions to ensure that these will accommodate the buying group vision.

IT initiatives may have to be reassessed to ensure that they are robust enough to meet the basic requirements that the newer applications demand in terms of response times, storage capacities, design flexibility and ease of integration with other platforms. Many such systems are able to integrate with other supporting IT applications such as supplier performance, technological measurement, critical path management, ordering, logistical and store systems.

Organisational hierarchical design must be guided by human resource expertise to enable the most efficient structures that will deliver the end in mind objectives.

A typical buying group organisation chart which is applied in the hypothetical CH Clothing Company is outlined below where the mainstream buying and merchandising function cascades down from the highest platform to the lower department level details. Service areas as depicted on the right hand side of the diagram support the core functions.

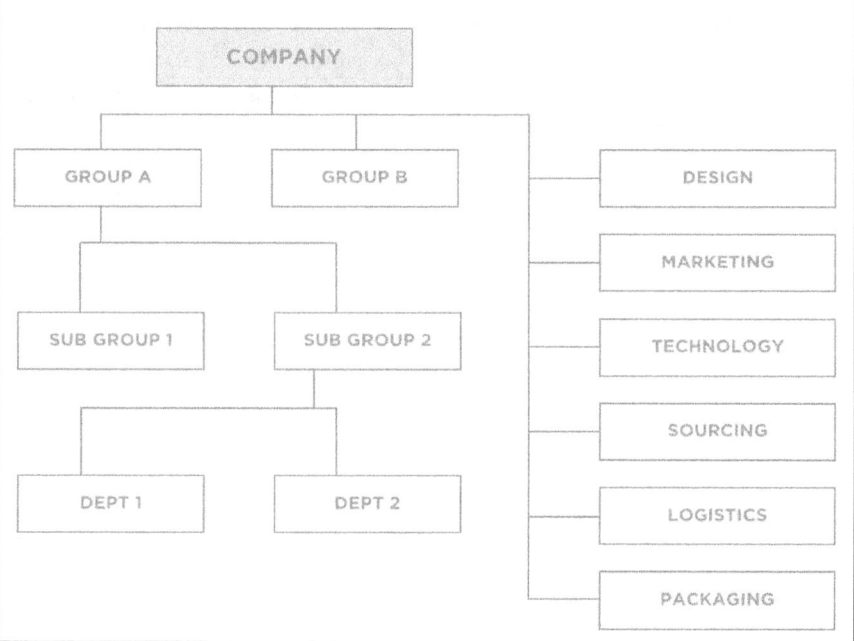

The basic hierarchical staffing roles of all the key players in a mainstream buying structure is outlined diagrammatically below.

The chief executive officer is clearly the leader together with the board of directors who ensure that the overall company strategic intent is delivered and the profits are achieved as reward to the shareholders to whom they are accountable.

Group executives look after the broad category types such as menswear, ladieswear and childrenswear. The responsibility is to ensure that the group delivers to the set strategy and is reacting properly to changing trading conditions while still meeting the profit objective.

Within the mainstream groups such as menswear a sub division into sub groups may well take place probably by lifestyle like formal wear and casual wear. The category manager is responsible for the mini business or sub group with set turnover targets, profit objectives and strategies.

Buyers, merchandisers and location planners operate at the departmental level down to the lowest degree of product being colour and size and are responsible that the management of the detail delivers the eventual goals at all the higher levels.

It must be emphasised that there is a very definitive collaborative process between the buying and merchandising team where an appropriate measure of tension may exist. The same environment may apply between the finance departments and the buying team in terms of the financial budget

Key staffing hierarchy posts of the buying organisation in the illustration of the hypothetical CH Clothing Company can be illustrated as follows

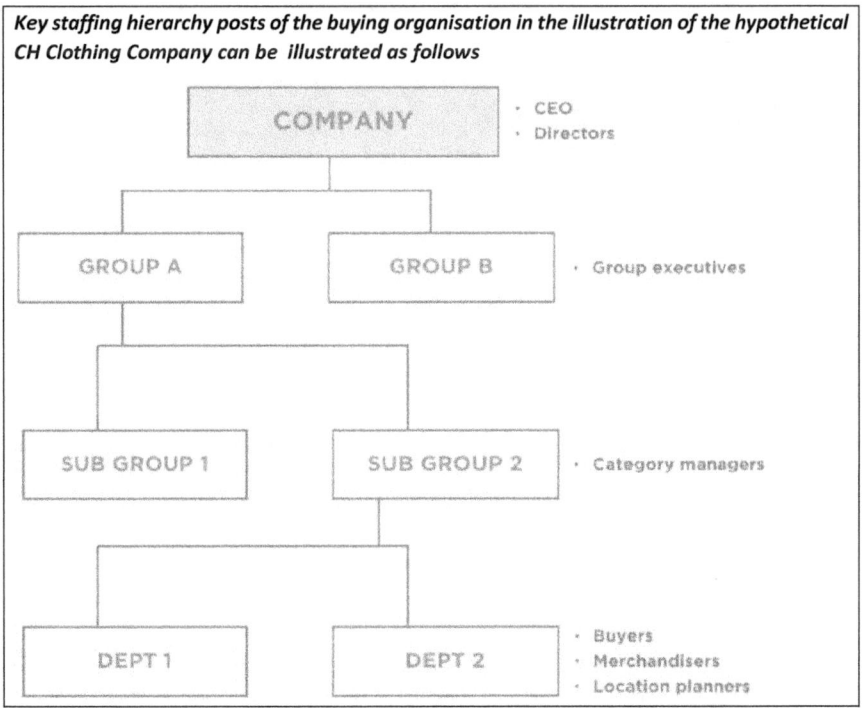

Customer strategy

Assuming that your customers are all the same is possibly the biggest error that could be made and the crucial part of growing any business is knowing intimately who your customers actually are.

Understanding the profile and lifestyle of the consumer very well is key to determine that the most appropriate product is developed to cater for the relevant customer segments and to ensure that the product information is effectively communicated through an integrated marketing plan and packaging policy.

Various factors have an influence on the profile of customers and knowledge of these will assist in the categorisation of customers and apply the most fitting methodologies that are a prerequisite to best serve them. Generally the typical segmentation of customers is determined by their behavioural needs, psychological characteristics and the environment wherein they exist. The strategic objective is to provide the customer with products that have a combination of integrity, quality and service, represent great value and create an enjoyable shopping experience in a pleasant environment that best suits the target market.

The key factors that influence the customer profiles are

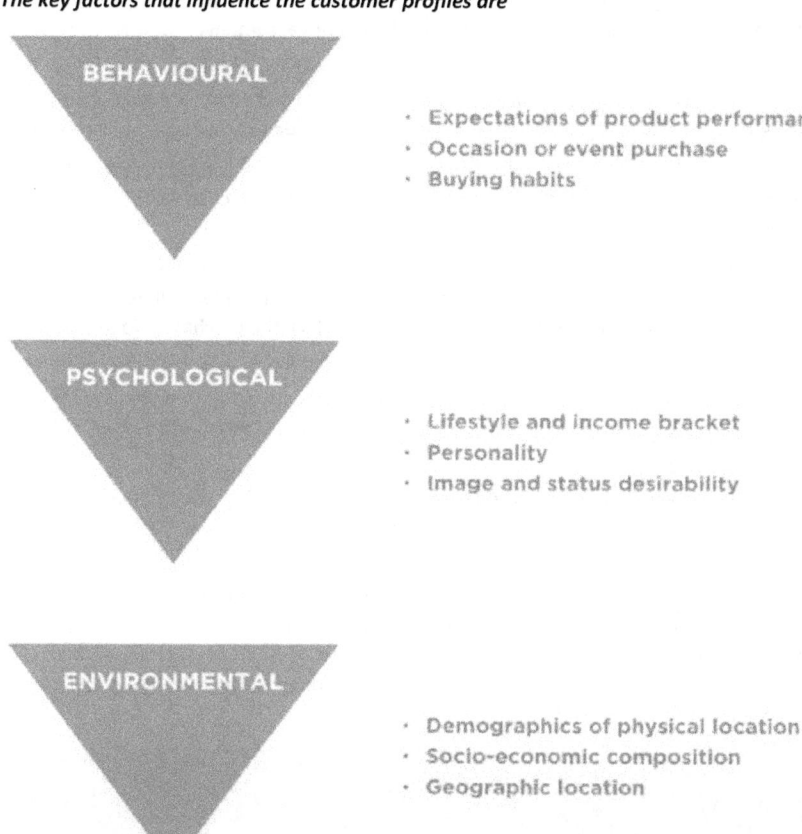

BEHAVIOURAL

· Expectations of product performance
· Occasion or event purchase
· Buying habits

PSYCHOLOGICAL

· Lifestyle and income bracket
· Personality
· Image and status desirability

ENVIRONMENTAL

· Demographics of physical location
· Socio-economic composition
· Geographic location

Behavioural influences are those that in the main are habitual and accommodate the personality traits of the customer. The motivating factor for making a purchase can be varied. A consumer may not be too influenced by the on trend level of the product but will possibly prefer to have an offering that will be durable, practical and functional. If these expectations are not met they will no doubt reject the product whereas at the other end of the scale these factors may be of lesser importance.

The potential customer could be more influenced by that which is socially acceptable and reflected in the media such as magazines, television and exhibited by role models like sports stars, actors and professional people who will play an important part of the selection process. The perception of fashion could differ considerably and therefore the fashion retailer will have to rely more and more heavily on practices that will assist in analysing their particular customer's profiles or that which characterises them more accurately.

Other behaviour traits possibly are where purchases are infrequent and will exist based on a need that a shopping experience will be more of a special assignment to acquire appropriate clothing for special occasions such as returning to work, weddings, holidays or sports events.

Buying habits may include the infrequent visit to stores in order to replace the entire wardrobe on a seasonal basis in order to remain relevant and replace those clothes that have reached their performance expiry date.

The satisfaction of psychological needs such as status and image is a strong motivator in the selection of the styles that will help to achieve this objective. Included will be the perceived expectation that needs to be met by the social circle in which the purchaser moves or reflects a level of wealth that is enjoyed.

There might be the natural drive to exploit the best bargains available and some shoppers may even develop a hobby out of pursuing the greatest values available at a maze of factory and value outlets.

Trawling the glitzy malls and frequenting coffee shops and eateries can be the past time that successfully satisfies the social interaction compulsion.

The more down to earth factors that influence the shopping patterns can be the geographical location where the customer resides. As an example is that a definite difference is detected in style preference between the urbanized to those who live in remoter places where the differing demographics have a probable direct relationship to the social economic environment particularly in terms of gender, occupation, age emphasis, household income and life stage.

Referring to the overall definition of the hypothetical CH Clothing Company we are able to compile a customer profile description in terms of the key influences of the overall company as follows

"CH Clothing Company is a respected mass fashion retailer selling mid-price quality product with a broad representation in malls, regional locations, city centres as well as supporting an on line facility offering core basic product supplemented by on trend mid fashion elements to capture a wide cross section of customer profiles"

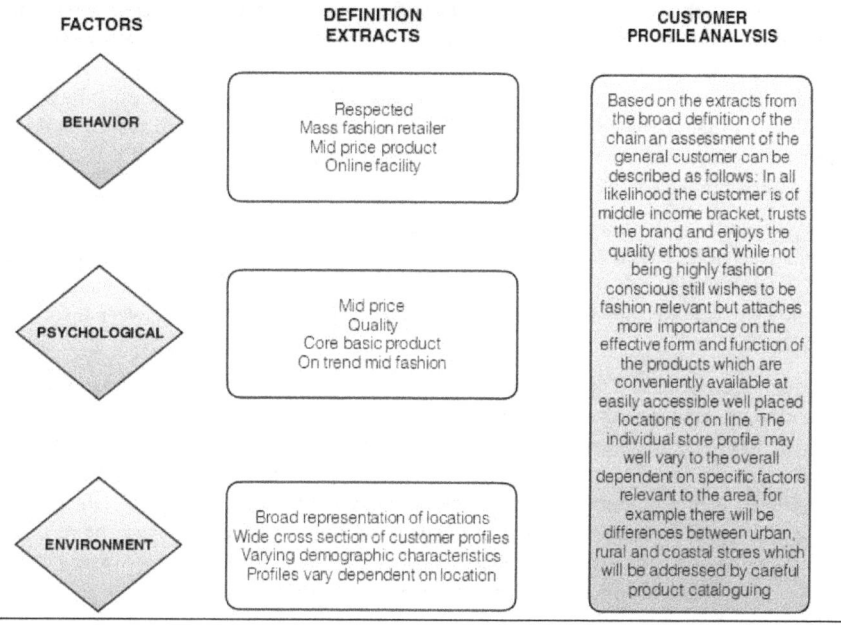

With the advance of till technology and the introduction of loyalty programmes it is now possible to gather a wealth of information that describes purchasing behaviour. The information that is harvested is the details of the product purchase such as style, colour, size, fit and price. The frequency and time of purchase and the relationship to other purchases can be analysed as well as the determination of the average spend per customer in different geographical areas is invaluable in building the profile of the customer base. What is of particular importance is the ability to assess the success of promotional launches and the impact they may have on other products during the time of the promotion.

It is no secret that people are living longer. There are some fundamental factors that need to be considered in terms of the population composition which needs to be taken into account in the longer term. A prime example is the greater number of older people who are still economically active at a much riper age. This is evident especially in the case of those individuals who were born at end of World War II when there was a significant baby boom and those babies are now embarking on their so called twilight years. With improved medical technology, healthier eating and lifestyles together with the explosion of health clubs as well as the trend to extend the years of economic activity has had the effect that the twilight years are going to be somewhat longer than in the past.

Another key factor is that the post war boomers enjoyed the availability of easy credit and a large number have accumulated high levels of debt with the result that when they should have been saving for their retirement years and reducing mortgages instead are landed in the situation that retirement is delayed or even worse some will have to continue working until their last. However, for the baby boomers those that are retiring are now fast approaching their retirement date if not already having experienced it. The impact of this is that there is a significant exodus of talent and work experience out of the market place and as such for those who are on the brink of retirement they are either encouraged to remain in the work place or venture into the consultancy pool.

Forensic auditing studies on mortality rate (SALT Table 1 – 1984-1986} compared in the National English tables for the period 2011 to 2013 showed that the mortality rate improved by 2.5% and 1.9% per annum for men and women respectively. Therefore the assumption can be drawn that a similar improvement going forward is likely to lie at least between these two extremes.

The impact on retailers is the need to make provision to accommodate the active aged in their store design. Store layouts will be required that are easy to shop with minimal confusion, lighting has to be bright and colour corrected to account for failing vision, noise levels need to be reduced to cater for the increased use of hearing aids, product weights must be considered and include an increased carry out service, font sizes need to be larger, shelf heights will have to be such to minimize bending and reaching while packaging should make for easier carrying and opening, queuing philosophies should be reviewed as well as the fitting rooms to permit the comfortable trying on of garments.

At the other end of the scale, the younger generations typically born in the seventies and eighties known as the millennial generation or generation Y are evolving into an extremely different personality to their predecessors and have become legendry in their prolific spending, their brand awareness and because they are technologically advanced this makes them more adventurous. Such characteristics may be evident in the pursuit of their career aspirations as they tend to progress through various places of employment while carving their career at a whim in contrast to their parents who often followed the same occupation for a lifetime. Because these cool, energetic participants are screen junkies they are easily influenced by social media trends and fads. They are therefore able to make informed comparisons and as a result the loyal practice of only shopping at one destination is almost non-existent which places a real test on the retailers to capture a core base market.

Marketing is left with an incredible task to innovate and communicate with this new breed of customer that is arriving on the scene at a rapid pace. Retailers have to start thinking like their customers as in place of window shopping this new breed trawls the internet and stays in contact all the time via the social channels and consequently the retailer need to ramp up their image amongst the channels through financial investment in top class copy writing and superb photographs as well as actively interact on line with their customer. The location of the on line sites should, as with bricks and mortar outlets, be in the best possible space where the greatest exposure to the target customer through the measurement of the number of click troughs is achieved. The offering must be easily found on websites that are advertised forcefully among local advertising vehicles, public relations efforts, promotions and word of mouth.

A popular trend emerging amongst digital enthusiasts is the support for blog sites where the brands are able to speak to an audience in a different light. There is a word of caution in that what they tell the people must be well accepted because should it be met with resistance the consequences could be equally disastrous. Examples exist of some successful fashion blogs that attract thirty thousand hits a day and may have up to two hundred thousand followers on twitter and therefore brands are happy to pay a lot of money to purchase advertising space in these forums. Some brands spend more than fifty percent of their advertising provision on electronic channels and collaborate with bloggers to gain the most editorial exposure. Many designers view the bloggers as their spokespersons as they develop strong relationships with customers by offering fashion tips and advice, the provision of educational material and programmes that help with the customer decision making process as well as at the same time enhancing brand awareness.

Product planning strategy

Once there is a clear understanding of what operational activities are required, the plan of action can be outlined to deliver the strategic objectives and thereby satisfy the goals of the strategy in the most effective way.

What is key in formulating the planning strategy is to set down the clear guidelines in the development of the product mix which will be carefully tailored in the right proportions in order to best serve the customer at the various locations and in terms of styling, colour quantities across the sizes at the most acceptable prices.

For this to be done successfully the overall process of planning follows a set of prescribed activities that make up the mechanics of running the business as well as accommodating the other stakeholder strategies. The steps are a flow of taking in the lessons learnt during the previous season and utilising the learnings as input in the formulation of the strategic goals for the future season.

The goals will give guidance in the preparation of the level of budgets determining the product mix and setting up the range plan from which the orders will be placed. Once production has taken place according to the plan the goods will be allocated to the stores taking into account their specific customer characteristics. Sales will be analysed as they occur and as the performance dictates the forward plans will be reviewed and adjusted appropriately.

Diagrammatically the high level key planning steps can be outlined as follows

Believe it or not the start of planning for a forthcoming season begins with what has happened in the past.

A strategic focus in the assessment of the past performance for the season is to compare the actual vital numbers to that what was expected and understand the deviations whether they were positive or negative. The learnings are imperative in the compilation of a new season's strategy and the setting of targets.

Once there is a clear understanding of what operational activities are required, the plan of action can be outlined to deliver the strategic objectives and thereby satisfy the goals of the strategy in the most effective way.

What is key in formulating the planning strategy is to set down the clear guidelines in the development of the product mix which will be carefully tailored in the right proportions in order to best serve the customer at the various locations and in terms of styling, colour quantities across the sizes at the most acceptable prices.

For this to be done successfully the overall process of planning follows a set of prescribed activities that make up the mechanics of running the business as well as accommodating the other stakeholder strategies. The steps are a flow of taking in the lessons learnt during the previous season and utilising the learnings as input in the formulation of the strategic goals for the future season.

The goals will give guidance in the preparation of the level of budgets determining the product mix and setting up the range plan from which the orders will be placed. Once production has taken place according to the plan the goods will be allocated to the stores taking into account their specific customer characteristics. Sales will be analysed as they occur and as the performance dictates the forward plans will be reviewed and adjusted appropriately.

CONCLUSION

While a lot has been documented on the subject of strategic planning, the proof of the pudding is in the eating in that the success of the plan is reflected in the sincerity, integrity and results that are delivered.

More often than not after a lot of effort and time by a number of people has been inputted in the formulation of the plan, unless it is applied, measured and adapted it is simply a waste. It is not uncommon for the strategic plan to be left on the shelf and the executive director carries on going in different directions without the board demanding fidelity to the agreed goals. While changing direction may be warranted, these should be carefully vetted and agreed by all stakeholders and the plan amended accordingly.

For this reason it is critical that disciplined check points are established where the actual performance of the plan is measured in terms of its efficiency, the actual deliverance compared to the targets set out, the quality and the flexibility of the plan to be able to adapt easily.

A key focus in the assessment of the past performance for the season is to compare the actual key numbers to that what was expected and understand the deviations whether they were positive or negative. The learnings are imperative in the compilation of a new season's strategy and setting of targets.

The key topics that need to be questioned and evaluated are:

Product

- Were the trends which were anticipated in line with what actually materialised? What needs to be taken into account when predicting the future season's trends?
- Did the strategy that was set for the brand and customer together with that of the group and department as well as the supplier selection deliver the envisaged objectives? What needs to be done differently for the new season?

Customers and competitors

- Did the information on customer segmentation and the action plans cater effectively in the satisfaction of the needs? What adaptations and additional resources are needed for the future season?

- Did the competitor initiatives which were anticipated actually happen and was it possible to effectively counteract them? What other methodologies are available to keep up to date with the market place activities?

Key performance indicators

- Were the targets of sales, margins, stock levels and turns, gross and net profits achieved as per plan or were they unrealistic? What measures require review and which activities are needed to be put in place to achieve them in the new season?
- Was the product assortment in the right proportions and did they perform to acceptable levels to cater for all customer segments effectively? Were the product innovations and promotions that were implemented successful and at the right levels?
- What were the actual colours and sizes sold in comparison to the volumes purchased and what should have been bought instead?
- Identify product sales which need to be adjusted to a realistic level as a result of product failure, poor availabilities and any other factors such as competitive activity and what special events were there that may have influenced sales either positively or negatively.

Suppliers

- Did the suppliers perform to the levels that maximised availability in the right quantities and on time?
- Did the selected suppliers possess the right capabilities to deliver the programmes that were allotted in terms of innovation, complexity, capacity, quality and on time delivery? Are there other suppliers who should be considered?
- Was the feedback received from suppliers of a nature that can help improve the working relationships going forward?

Stores

- Were stores able to understand the structure of the ranges and easily display them to emphasize the thinking of the buying team? What improvements to guidelines can be made to assist them?
- Was the feedback received from stores valuable and what mechanisms can be implemented to improve the quality of feedback?

Marketing

- Were the marketing channels that were utilised effective and was the uplift in sales able to be measured accurately against control products? Which other communication mediums would be considered?
- Were the promotions successful and what was the extent of substitution purchases?
- What was the feedback from store staff and customers?
- Were the social initiative objectives achieved?

In the final analysis if the responses to the above evaluation points are positive one can safely say that an effective strategy was applied. If some of the results were not as those that were expected the key is to take the lessons learnt on board and focus on them in the preparation for future seasons.

In summary, having a farsighted view of the overall big picture of the retail environment, with an all-inclusive attention to detail and being aware of early warning signs to effectively avoid challenges through the optimised use of the tools, mechanisms and talents at hand is without doubt a key factor in delivering a successful and sustainable retail business.